BE A MAGICIAN

BY
Ali Bongo
ILLUSTRATED BY
Kate Charlesworth

MACDONALD

First published 1979
Reprinted 1980

Macdonald Educational Ltd
Holywell House
Worship Street
London EC2A 2EN

Printed by New Interlitho,
Milan, Italy

About this book

This book has been carefully planned to help you become an expert. Look for the special pages to find the information you need. **RECOGNITION** pages, with a **bright pink flash** in the top right-hand corner, contain all the essential information to know and remember. **PROJECT** pages, with a **grey border,** suggest some interesting ideas for things to do and make. At the end of the book there is a useful **REFERENCE SECTION**.

So you want to be a magician

Wouldn't it be marvellous if you could make things disappear, or change, or float in the air at your command? By using simple yet crafty methods, a magician can make these things look as if they are really happening.

Today the secrets of magic are used mainly for entertainment; to make people laugh as well as wonder. In this book you will learn some of these secrets.

The variety of magic
There is more to magic than just performing tricks. You can make your own props, invent tricks of your own and collect magic books and old apparatus.

Find out whether there is a magic club in your area. It is the best way to meet other magicians and to learn new tricks.

People have always been fascinated – and sometimes frightened – by the power of magic.

The Balancing Egg
Hide a small pile of salt under the tablecloth before you start. Choose an egg and press it down on top of the pile to make it stand upright.

salt cellar

salt

Is magic easy to do?
Nearly all the best tricks are based on very simple methods. The difficult part is learning how to present them. What counts is not what you do but the way that you do it.

Misleading the audience
Take this simple trick of balancing an egg upright on the table. You could go straight ahead and just do it – which is clever but rather boring. Or you could examine a whole heap of eggs, one by one, holding them up and pretending to look for 'the right one'.

This will puzzle your audience far more. They will think there is something special about the actual egg you choose, and never guess how the trick is done.

The variety of magic

There are lots of different kinds of magic – some of which are illustrated here.

Of course most magicians know more than one type of magic. Having tried them all, they specialize in the one that they enjoy most, or are best at.

▶Manipulation
Manipulators use only the skill of their hands (or 'sleight-of-hand') to perform tricks. They use cards, billiard balls, thimbles and other small objects.

◀Mental magic
This type of magician is called a mentalist or mind-reader. He reads other people's thoughts and predicts the future.

▼Tricks with doves
This type of magic is a branch of manipulation. The performer produces doves, parrots, pigeons, or even poodles.

►Illusions
This is often the most spectacular magic of all. The illusionist uses larger animals like tigers and elephants, and performs amazing tricks with people – often volunteers from the audience.

▼General magic
This type of performer uses all kinds of small apparatus and works on a stage.

▼Close-up magic
This is the best kind of magic for the beginner and can be performed anywhere.

Where to start

▲A mentalist or mind-reader

As you have already discovered, there are lots of different kinds of magic. You may have decided that one day you will be a famous illusionist – or a mind-reader and amazing predictor of the future, like the man in the picture above.

Close-up magic

The best way to start, though, is with close-up magic because much of it uses ordinary household objects, like the egg in the balancing trick on page 5.

Close-up magic is also very popular because, like this sugar lump trick, it looks much more difficult than other magic as it is performed right under the spectators' noses.

The Vanishing Sugar Lumps

First, drape a paper napkin over your half-closed fist. Then, with the fingers of your other hand, push down the centre of the napkin to make a 'well' **(1)**.

Drop two sugar lumps into the well and sprinkle some salt over the napkin. Then say *'Hey presto – sugar go!'* and quickly tear up the napkin into small pieces, showing that the sugar lumps have disappeared.

The secret is: that you really push a hole right through the paper and then let the sugar lumps fall through it on to your lap as you reach for the salt-cellar **(2).**

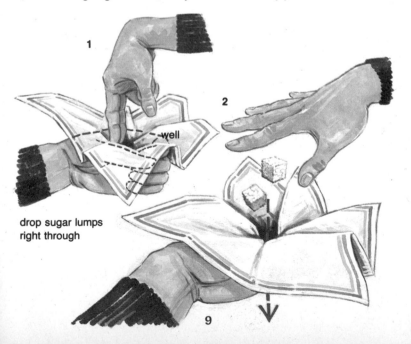

1

well

2

drop sugar lumps
right through

9

Close-up tricks

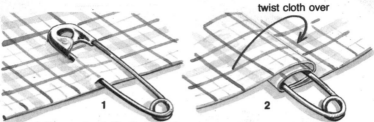

twist cloth over

The Liberated Safety-Pin

Place a cotton handkerchief on the table and fold it in half. Now pin both sides of the cloth together with a large safety pin, about 1cm from the edge **(1).**

Wrap some of the cloth around one end of the pin by twisting it over gently three times **(2).**

Press down on the cloth just beyond the covered end of the pin. Then grip the other end tightly and pull it smoothly away from the handkerchief.

The pin will slide out easily – and still be closed!

Dice Divination

You will need: an empty matchbox and two dice which fit snugly into it; they must be able to rattle but **not** turn over.

Now ask someone to shake the box, turn it upside down on the table and slide out the drawer.

Without lifting the drawer you will be able to tell him the numbers on top of the dice.
The secret is: remember that numbers on the opposite sides of all dice add up to seven.

So just remember the numbers on top when you put the dice into the box and then subtract them from seven.

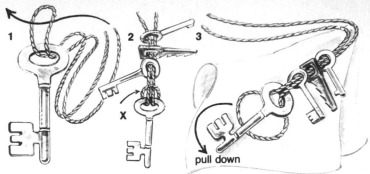

pull down

The Escaping Keys

You will need: four or five keys and a length of string.

Double the string and push the loop through the end of the largest key. Then pass both ends of the string through the loop and pull tight **(1)**.

Now thread the ends of the string through the other keys **(2)** and ask someone to hold them for you.

Cover the keys with a handkerchief. Then pull down on the loop marked '**X**' to release the big key.

Quickly remove the other keys from the string, then replace the big key by looping the string back over it and pulling tight.

Produce the loose keys one by one, then remove the handkerchief to show everyone that the big key is still firmly knotted to the string.

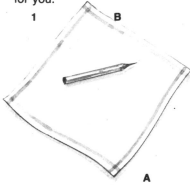

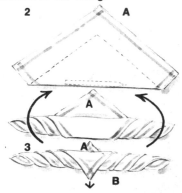

The Penetrating Pencil

Place a handkerchief diagonally on the table, with corner '**A**' nearest to you as shown **(1)**. Lay a pencil on it just beyond the centre.

Fold corner '**A**' so that it slightly overlaps corner '**B**' **(2)**.

Then roll up the pencil in the handkerchief until corner '**B**' appears again.

Hold onto corner '**A**' with one hand and pull '**B**' back towards you with the other **(3)**.

The pencil is now **underneath** the handkerchief – amazing isn't it?

11

More close-up tricks

The Vanishing Coin

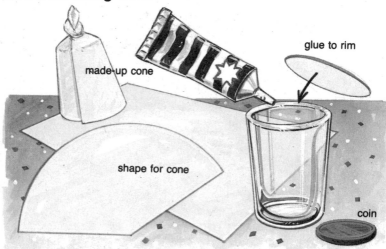

glue to rim

made-up cone

shape for cone

coin

Preparation
You will need: a small glass (a medicine glass is ideal), two identical sheets of thick, coloured paper, glue, and a pair of scissors.

Draw around the mouth of an upturned glass, then cut out the circle you have made. Glue it to the rim of the glass.

Cut the rest of the paper to the shape illustrated above and make a cone that covers the glass completely.

Performance
Place the glass upside-down on the second sheet of paper – no one will notice the glued-on circle because both bits of paper are the same colour.

Now put a small coin onto the paper and tell your audience that you are going to make it disappear.

Cover the glass with the cone, lift both together and put them on top of the coin. Now say some magic words and lift up the cone – the coin will have disappeared!

It is of course simply hidden by the paper circle, but your audience won't guess that.

To make the coin come back, place the cone over the glass and lift them both up together.

Never move the glass without covering it, and always have another, unprepared glass ready to confuse a suspicious audience.

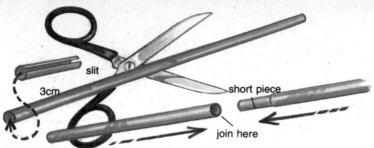

The Cut and Restored Straw

Preparation

Cut a 3cm piece from a plastic drinking straw and slit it down the middle. Then squeeze it into the end of another straw, leaving about 1cm sticking out.

Performance

Cut the straw in two, then wave both halves in the air to prove that it really has been cut.

Say some magic words and push the end of the short bit into the other half of the straw. It will hold both halves together.

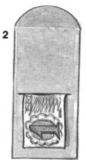

The Indestructible Note

Preparation

Take a long brown envelope (the kind that opens at one end) and cut a slit across the back (1).

Then just below it cut a small cross through both the front and the back.

Performance

Hold the envelope with the slit towards you. Slide a banknote into it, making sure that the bottom end comes through the slit at the back (2). Then secretly fold it upwards (3).

Pick up a pencil and push it through the cross-cut – so that it looks as if you are going right through the note (4).

Then quickly pull the note out of the envelope – it is of course completely unharmed!

A magician's hands

An audience is always watching a magician's hands; they are the tools of his trade. So it is very important to keep them looking good and working well.

Finger-suppling exercises
The best way to improve your flexibility and co-ordination is by doing regular finger exercises like the ones described below.

Finger exercises

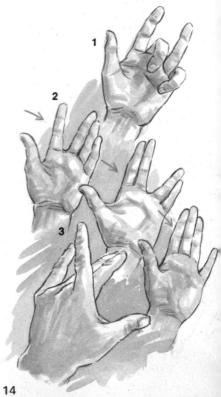

1. Close your fingers tightly into your palm, then open them one by one, starting with the forefinger.
   Then try opening alternate fingers: second finger, little finger, forefinger, third finger and so on.

2. Hold your hand up straight and separate your fingers as illustrated on the left. Now change positions as quickly as you can.

3. Touch the tip of your little finger with the tip of your forefinger – first at the back, then quickly at the front.

14

The Floating Sausage

sausage

Hold your forefingers together as shown (1), about 10cm away from your eyes. Don't stare too hard and you will see what looks like a little pink sausage in between your finger tips.

Separate your fingers slightly and the 'sausage' will seem to float in the air (2).

The Stretching Finger

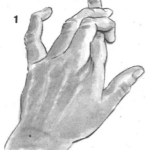

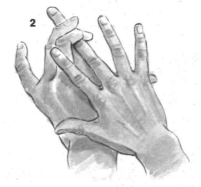

First tuck your left forefinger under your second and third fingers (1).

Then push your right middle finger in on top (2).

It will look as if you are stretching your right middle finger with your left hand.

The Third Forefinger

Hold your left forefinger about 20cm away from your nose and stare at it very hard.

Now put your right forefinger about 20cm beyond your left, so that your fingers and nose form a straight line.

Keep on looking hard at the left finger. You should now be able to see **two** right fingers – one on each side of your left.

straight line

Card tricks

How to find a chosen card

trim off 1mm

glue

In many card tricks, a magician has to keep track of a card selected by a member of the audience. Here's one easy way to do it.

Preparation
Take the two jokers from your pack and glue them neatly together. Then carefully trim 1mm off one end to make a short thick card. Place it face down on top of the pack.

Performance
Fan out the cards for someone to choose one. Ask them to remember it and put it back on top of the pack. Then cut the pack a few times.

(Remember, cutting does not change the order of the cards – the chosen card will stay next to the thick card.)

Finally, hold the pack face down, and cut it exactly at the thick card (see below). This brings the thick card to the top and the chosen card to the bottom of the pack.

Without showing it, put the pack in your pocket and use your 'sensitive finger tips' to bring out the chosen card.

thick card

side-view of pack

How to force a card

You may sometimes need to make someone choose the card you want them to without them realizing it. This is called 'forcing a card'.

One way to do it is like this: place the card you want to be chosen on top of the pack. Then ask someone to cut the pack and place the lower half **(A)** at right angles across the upper half **(B)**, in order to 'mark the cut'.

Now you must chat for a few moments so that he forgets which half is which. (This is a method of distracting the audience that all magicians use, called 'patter'.)

Then ask him to lift off the top pack **(A)** and look at the top card of the lower pack **(B)**. As this was the original top card of the pack you have successfully 'forced' the card.

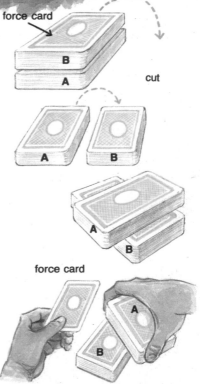

force card

cut

force card

The Enchanted Card Box

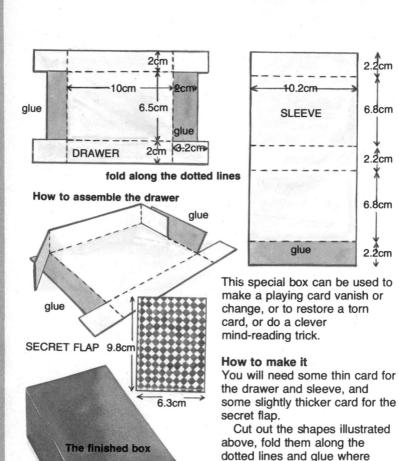

fold along the dotted lines

2cm
—10cm—
2cm
6.5cm
2cm
glue
glue
DRAWER
2cm
3.2cm

2.2cm
—10.2cm—
SLEEVE
6.8cm
2.2cm
6.8cm
glue
2.2cm

How to assemble the drawer

glue

glue

SECRET FLAP 9.8cm

6.3cm

The finished box

This special box can be used to make a playing card vanish or change, or to restore a torn card, or do a clever mind-reading trick.

How to make it

You will need some thin card for the drawer and sleeve, and some slightly thicker card for the secret flap.

Cut out the shapes illustrated above, fold them along the dotted lines and glue where indicated.

Cover the outsides of the sleeve and drawer with plain coloured paper. Line the inside of the drawer with a paper that has a small, fussy pattern.

The secret flap should be covered in the same paper and should fit loosely into the bottom of the drawer.

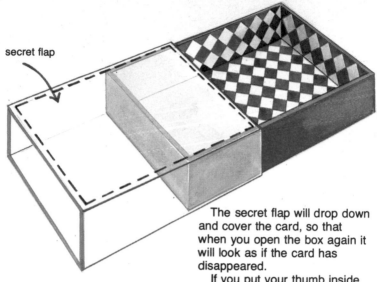

secret flap

The Vanishing Card

Preparation
Open the drawer nearly all the way, and insert the secret flap between the top edge of the drawer and the cover – as shown by the dotted line in the diagram above. Make sure it is completely out of sight.

Performance
Take a card from your pack and show it to the audience, drop it into the box and close the drawer.

The secret flap will drop down and cover the card, so that when you open the box again it will look as if the card has disappeared.

If you put your thumb inside to stop the flap from falling out, you can even pull the drawer right out and turn it upside down.

Then spread the pack face down on the table and reveal the missing card, face up in the middle of the spread.

How to do it
Take a duplicate card from another pack and turn it over in the middle of your pack before you start the trick.

the missing card

The Changing Card

Preparation
This is the same as for the **Vanishing Card,** except that you also place a card face down on top of the secret flap.

Performance
Show the audience a different card and then place it face down in the box.

Close the box carefully, making sure that the secret flap and the hidden card drop down together to cover the card you showed the audience.

Say some magic words and open the box again. Take out the card and show everyone that it has mysteriously changed.

The Torn and Restored Card

Preparation
For this trick you will need two duplicate cards. Place one on top of the secret flap, and the other in your pack, ready to be forced on someone in the audience (see page 17).

Performance
Ask for a volunteer and force the card on him. Then ask him to tear it into quarters. Put the pieces into the box and close it. When you reopen the box, the card is in one piece again!

20

The Rising Card

One of the most famous card tricks in the world is the **Rising Card.** Here is one of the easiest ways to do it.

Preparation
Cut a hole in the back of your card case as shown **(1).** Then place your special thick card on top of the pack.

Performance
Ask someone to choose a card, then replace it on top of the pack and cut the pack several times.

Wave your magic wand over the top of the case, then very slowly push up the chosen card with your thumb **(3).**

Remove the card to show that it really is the selected one.

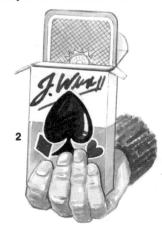

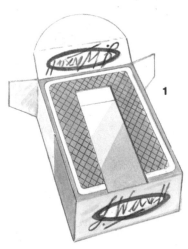

Take the pack back and cut it again, this time at the thick card, so that the chosen card goes to the bottom. Hold the card case with the cut-out underneath and slide the pack into it, face down.

Pick up the case as shown **(2),** keeping the cut-out side away from the audience.

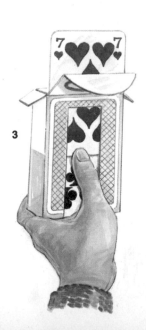

A programme for close-up magic

Now that you've learned some close-up tricks, you will probably want to put on a show.

You will always perform better if you have worked out the programme beforehand and practised it several times. Here is one idea for a show, but you can easily make up a programme of your own.

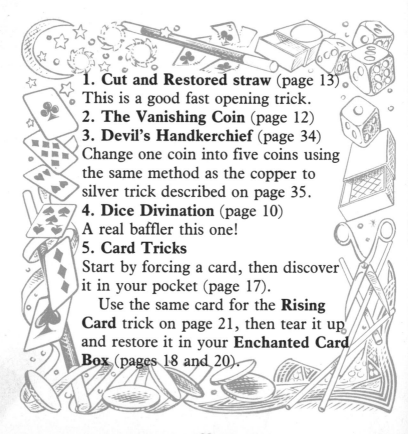

1. Cut and Restored straw (page 13)
This is a good fast opening trick.
2. The Vanishing Coin (page 12)
3. Devil's Handkerchief (page 34)
Change one coin into five coins using the same method as the copper to silver trick described on page 35.
4. Dice Divination (page 10)
A real baffler this one!
5. Card Tricks
Start by forcing a card, then discover it in your pocket (page 17).
Use the same card for the **Rising Card** trick on page 21, then tear it up and restore it in your **Enchanted Card Box** (pages 18 and 20).

A performance of close-up magic.

Close-up magic usually takes place with the magician standing behind a table and the spectators seated around the other three sides.

A close-up mat and props-box
Always cover your table, to avoid damaging it. Many magicians use a close-up mat to work on. You can easily make one for yourself out of thick felt, fabric-backed sponge or even thin carpet.

Don't keep all your props on the table while you're performing. Put them in a box, which you can keep on a chair beside you. This box will also be useful for getting rid of anything 'suspicious'.

Involving the audience
Always remember to look at each spectator in turn, making sure that everyone sees important things like the face of a chosen card or the numbers on the dice.

Close-up apparatus

▲**The Ball Vase.** With this magic vase, you can make the little red ball keep on vanishing and reappearing.

▲**The Magic Paddles,** or 'Dotty Spots'. The little black spots appear, disappear and hop from one paddle to the other.

▲**Colour Vision.** The magician correctly names the colour chosen by a spectator.

▲**Grandmother's Necklace.** The shiny wooden beads can be mysteriously released from the string.

▲**Cups and Sponges.** This is a miniature and easier version of the classic Cups and Balls trick.

These are some of the tricks that you will find in magic stores and conjuring sets from toy shops. With a little practice you will find that they are all quite easy to do.

▲**Acrobatic Matchbox.** It can creep, crawl, stand up and open all by itself, on your hand.

▼**Imp Bottle.** A lively little bottle that will only lie down at the magician's command.

▼**Nest of Boxes.** A marked coin vanishes, then is surprisingly discovered in a small bag, inside a set of boxes.

Party magic

The tangerine touch is always a popular party trick.

If your friends have enjoyed your table-top magic, they may ask you to put on a show at a party.

At small parties you can perform close-up magic, but if there are lots of people you should put on a proper stage act.

Tips to remember

There will always be people who will ask you to keep on doing more and more tricks. But it is much better to do a short routine, finishing with a really strong effect. Then you can save some of your surprises for the next party.

Remember that the most popular tricks are those in which the spectators take part. The two tricks opposite are always a great success.

Tangerine Touch

Pass round a plate with some tangerines on it. When the audience has examined them, ask somebody to choose one and hand it to you.

Using a felt-tip or ballpoint pen, mark it with a cross. Now ask someone to tip all the tangerines into a paper bag, mix them thoroughly and hand it to you behind your back.

Then, even though you can't see inside the bag, you reach in and produce the marked tangerine.

How to do it
The secret is very simple. As you are marking the tangerine, give it a good squeeze. Then, when you are searching for it later, just feel for the softest one. You could even be blindfolded for this trick.

The silent spell will baffle all your friends!

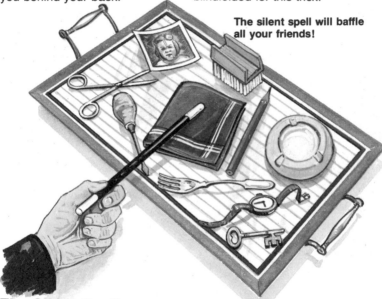

The Silent Spell

Preparation
First gather these articles together on a tray: **1.** key; **2.** fork; **3.** watch; **4.** pencil; **5.** ashtray; **6.** scissors; **7.** nailbrush; **8.** photograph; **9.** screwdriver; **10.** handkerchief.

Performance
Ask someone to choose an object and then spell its name silently to themselves, in time to your tapping objects on the tray – one letter for each tap. Tell them to stop you on the last letter; you will be pointing at what they have just spelt!

How it works
Just tap anything for the first two taps, then **follow the order on the list,** starting with the key.

27

Pop Goes the Lollipop!

Preparation
Fix a small cellophane-wrapped lollipop securely to one end of a 40cm piece of elastic. Pin the other end up your sleeve.

40cm

pin elastic here

paper bag

Performance
Secretly pull the lollipop out of your sleeve and hold it so that the elastic is hidden behind your wrist.

Show the audience the lollipop, then pretend to drop it into a paper bag while really letting the elastic pull it back up your sleeve.

Now blow up the paper bag and burst it – the lollipop has vanished!

Magnetic Cards

Arrange some playing cards on the table with your hand resting on top of them. When you lift up your hand all the cards stick to it as if magnetic!

How it works
It's all done with the help of a special card made by fixing a loop of fine thread (invisible sewing nylon or fishing line) through two holes in the card. Reinforce it by glueing another card to its face **(1)**.

Insert your middle finger through the loop, put the card flat on the table, then slip more cards in between the fake card and your fingers. Then gently lift up all the cards **(2)**.

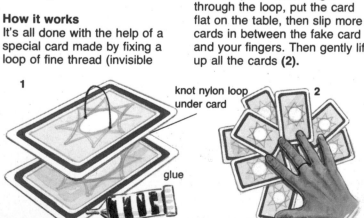

1

knot nylon loop under card

glue

2

How to make a stretching wand

You will need a length of wooden dowel about 40cm long and 1cm in diameter. Paint the ends white and the middle glossy black.

Now make an extra white end by rolling a strip of white paper 5cm by 10cm into a tube and glueing it securely. This fake end should fit closely around the wand, but still be able to slide up and down.

Performance
Start with the tube half-way along the wand, and with part of the wand hidden in your sleeve.

Pull on the other end, saying that your wand is too short and that you want to stretch it. Let the hidden part come slowly out of your sleeve. It will look as if the wand is getting longer. Let the fake end slip right off and keep it hidden in your hand until you can secretly get rid of it.

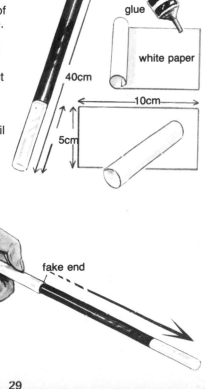

glue

white paper

40cm

10cm

5cm

hidden part

fake end

The classics of magic

Some tricks are so popular with an audience that they have become classics, and can be found in many magic acts. Most of these tricks depend on a secret which is built into the apparatus. You can buy them all from magic suppliers (see page 60).

◀**The Dove Pan.** With this magic pan, you can produce birds or even rabbits out of thin air.

▲**The Evaporated Milk Jug.** Milk is poured into a paper cone and then mysteriously vanishes.

◀**Ghost Tube.** An empty paper-capped tube is suddenly filled with handkerchiefs and brightly coloured ribbons.

▼The Chinese Rice Bowls. The grains of rice first double in quantity, then change into water.

▶The Linking Rings. Solid steel rings can be joined and then separated again.

▼Chinese Sticks. The strings at the ends of these bamboo sticks are quite separate, yet seem to be strangely connected.

▶The Sliding Dice Box. With this trick, you can make a solid block disappear from inside the box. It is later discovered in an empty hat!

31

Party challenges

Here are some more tricks for informal parties where everyone likes to join in. These crafty stunts or brain-teasers are not really magic, but they will certainly entertain your friends.

▲Arrange five glasses in a row, then fill the middle three with lemonade. Ask if anyone can rearrange the glasses so that they are alternately full and empty – but only by moving or touching **one** glass.

When they all give up, just pick up the middle glass, drink all the lemonade and put the glass back in the middle again!

drop it like this

◄Ask your friends to try and drop a full box of matches from about 20cm above the table so that it lands on one end – and stays standing upright.

This is almost impossible to do unless you first open the drawer slightly, then drop it as shown in the picture.

►Now produce a cup and a round balloon. Ask if anyone can lift the cup using only the balloon and without touching either the cup or its handle.

The only way to do it is to hold the balloon just inside the cup, and gently blow it up.

The balloon will grip the cup enough for it to be lifted.

Instant Cola

This is a very popular trick. First you pour a tumbler full of water into a china jug – when you pour it out again it has changed into sparkling cola! Hand it out to prove that it is genuine.

Using the system described below, you could transform water into milk or chunks of ice or even toffees – now that **would** be popular!

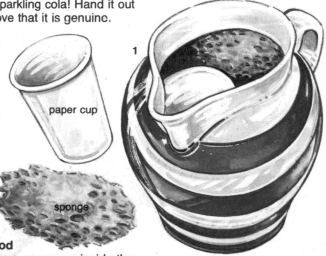

paper cup

sponge

Method
Wedge a paper cup inside the jug, close against the lip, using a bath sponge, cotton wool or anything that is absorbent **(1)**.

Fill the paper cup with cola, and have a glass of water nearby.

Simply pour the water into the sponge part of the jug – carefully avoiding the cup **(2)**.

The sponge will soak up the water, so that when you pour out again only the cola flows into the glass **(3)**.

The Devil's Handkerchief

You will need two large identical handkerchiefs, with a strong detailed pattern. Place one on top of the other.

Sew them carefully together, following the dotted lines in the picture exactly **(1)**, and leaving corners **A** and **B** free to form a secret pocket. Use it for vanishing small objects like coins, cards, dice or sweets.

How to use it
1. Make the handkerchief into a bag by gathering the corners into one hand – except for one corner of the secret pocket.

3. Take hold of both corners of the pocket with your other hand, say some magic words and shake out the handkerchief **(3)**. Pull it loosely through your free hand to show that the object has really vanished.

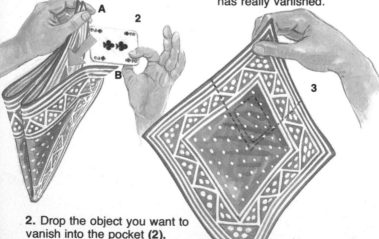

2. Drop the object you want to vanish into the pocket **(2)**.

Five tricks with the Devil's Handkerchief

1. Ask someone to choose a card, then make it vanish in the handkerchief and reappear in your **Enchanted Card Box.** You will need two identical cards for this trick – see the **Torn and Restored Card** on page 20 for the preparation.

2. Have the handkerchief already folded into a bag with a silver coin inside it – but **not** in the secret pocket. Ask someone for a copper coin, drop it in the pocket, then gently shake out the handkerchief. The copper coin has turned to silver!

3. Show the audience both sides of the 'empty' handkerchief. Then say some magic words and pour sweets from it onto a plate.

Before you start, hide the sweets in the secret pocket.

4. Using the same system as in **(2)**, you can make separate paper clips join together in a chain. The chain is inside the folded handkerchief at the start and the loose clips go inside the pocket.

5. Tear up a picture or photograph and make the pieces vanish in the handkerchief. Then make the picture reappear, fully restored, in the **Magic Picture Frame** (see page 48).

35

A programme for a party

Now that you've learned some good tricks for
parties, you are ready to put on a show for your
friends. Here is one idea for a party programme but
you can easily think up one of your own.

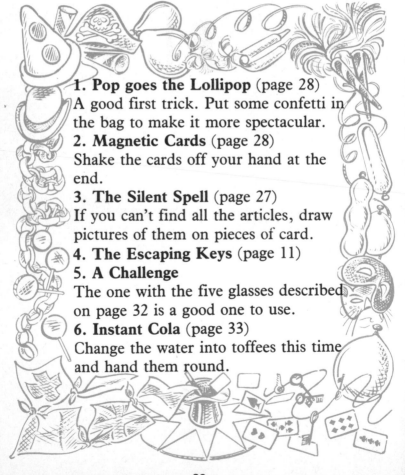

1. Pop goes the Lollipop (page 28)
A good first trick. Put some confetti in
the bag to make it more spectacular.
2. Magnetic Cards (page 28)
Shake the cards off your hand at the
end.
3. The Silent Spell (page 27)
If you can't find all the articles, draw
pictures of them on pieces of card.
4. The Escaping Keys (page 11)
5. A Challenge
The one with the five glasses described
on page 32 is a good one to use.
6. Instant Cola (page 33)
Change the water into toffees this time
and hand them round.

Design a magic poster

Always work it out carefully on thin paper first. Then rub over the back of the paper with a soft pencil (1), and lay it over the poster paper.

Now go over the lines with a hard pencil. Press hard enough for the design to be transferred (2).

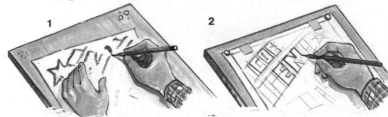

Fill in the design with poster paints (3). Use a felt-tip for the smaller lettering. The word **MAGIC** should always be in capital letters so that everybody notices it.

Use a simple design like cards, hands or a rabbit, and don't use too many colours. A combination of bright red, yellow and black is one of the most effective.

Invent your own magic

Magic is like music. There are eight basic notes in music, which can be arranged in millions of different ways to make new tunes. Magic has certain principles which can be applied to all sorts of objects in different combinations to create new tricks.

Using the basic principles
First you must learn as many of these principles as possible. You've already learnt about secret flaps in the **Enchanted Card Box** and hidden pockets in the **Devil's Handkerchief** – how then could you apply these principles to other objects?

Secret flaps can be used in picture frames, as you will see, and you can even make secret pockets in a newspaper. Write down the principles in this book. Now see how many new tricks you can invent.

A secret notebook

Reverse the notebook to make a second type of record.

Use a thick exercise book to keep a record of all your performances. Write down:
1. place, date and time of show;
2. how long it lasted;
3. the tricks you did, in order (note the most popular ones);
4. type of audience – ages and numbers;
5. anything that went wrong or that needs to be changed or practised.

Turn the book over and start a different kind of record at the back. Write down:
1. all the tricks you know and can do well;
2. the props required for each one;
3. the routine and patter;
4. how long each trick takes;
5. any ideas for new tricks – perhaps ones you have seen or read about.

A typical page.

Stage costumes

A colourful costume can make all the difference to your stage show. All these costumes are easy to make, using materials found around the house.

►If you own a happycoat or a kimono-style dressing-grown, you could dress up as a Chinese conjurer. Wear a length of material as a 'skirt' under it.

Chinese conjurer

head-dress

Modern magician

▲A girl could wear this costume with a flowered head-dress in place of the mandarin hat.

60cm

▲The modern magician wears a black shirt and trousers. You can make the bow tie and sash with a length of red material.

▲To make a cape, cut a piece of black material to the shape illustrated above.

An 'Arabian nights' costume

The wizard

▲Borrow some large pyjama trousers and tuck them into your socks to make baggy pants. Tie a sash around your waist and wear an earring or curtain ring!

▲The gown is a simple T-shape (see below). Decorate it with shapes made out of silver foil.

turban

gown

▲Ask your mother if she has an old hat which you can make into a fez or turban.

On the stage

When the curtains open and you walk out on stage, the first thing that everyone will notice is your appearance. Magicians are expected to look smart, so whatever costume you decide to wear, make sure that it is clean and well-pressed.

Exits and entrances
Walk briskly to the centre of the stage as soon as you are announced, smile to acknowledge the applause and start your act immediately.

Your exit is just as important; take your time to smile and bow. If you have performed well you should come back on stage for another bow – but only if the audience is still applauding.

◄A professional magician always wears theatrical make-up to make him look natural under the strong lights.

▲Even an amateur magician should always look clean and smart. Being well-groomed will help to give you confidence.

Your props

Props with matt colours and no fussy decorations are best; they will look good from the front row and still be clearly visible from the back.

Stage lighting

It is a good idea to have spot-lights if you can, but remember that strong lighting can change the appearance of things. Take care with shiny metal apparatus and glossy paint – it may reflect the light and be difficult to see properly.

Stage lighting can also affect the way **you** look, as it drains the colour from your face. You will look like a ghost unless you wear theatrical make-up. Ask your drama teacher to show you how to use it.

Stage tricks

Confetti Candle

A candle stands in a candlestick on your table. You light it and let it burn while you make a cone out of a sheet of newspaper. You then blow out the candle, remove it from its holder and drop it into the cone.

With a wave of your magic wand, you turn the cone upside down and out pours a shower of confetti. When you crush up the cone, the candle has gone!

The assembled candle

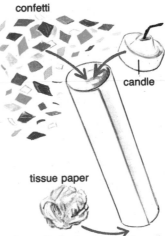

confetti

candle

tissue paper

Preparation
Make a fake candle out of a tube of stiff white paper and fill it with confetti. Stick a piece of

real candle in the top end and some tissue paper into the bottom to stop the confetti coming out too soon.

Performance
Drop the candle head-first into the cone so that you can grip it as you shake out the confetti.

Crush the fake candle and the cone together at the end.

The Magic Changing Bag

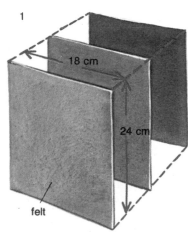

1

18 cm

24 cm

felt

The magic changing bag is used for vanishing, producing and exchanging one object for another. It is also useful for forcing a choice of colour or number in mind-reading tricks.

How to make it
You will need three pieces of dark coloured felt about 18cm by 24cm **(1).**

Place them on top of each other and sew the edges around three sides to form a bag with two separate compartments **(2).**

Add a border round the top of the bag with some coloured ribbon or gold braid **(3).**

gold braid

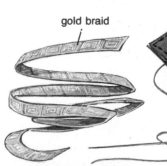

2

3

How to use it
With an object concealed in one side of the bag, you can turn the other compartment inside out to show that the bag is apparently empty.

You will find other ways to use it described elsewhere in the book.

More stage magic

The Vanishing Tumbler

You need: a plastic tumbler, two patterned handkerchiefs, and a disc of cardboard the size of the top of the tumbler.

Sew the disc inside the two handkerchiefs **(A)**. Another square of stitching **(B),** will keep it in place in the centre.

Cover the table with a thick tablecloth pulled well down at the back and pinned up to make a large open pocket, deep enough to hold the tumbler.

Performance

Cover the tumbler with the handkerchief, so the disc fits on top of the rim. Then, holding it at the top, slide it backwards off the edge of the table so that it slips down out of the handkerchief and into the pocket.

Hold the disc so that the tumbler seems to be still there. Take it nearer the audience, then shake out the handkerchief to show that it has vanished.

The tumbler drops easily into the pocket.

The Flying Silks

This trick is based on the **Vanishing Tumbler,** but is even more spectacular and colourful.

Besides the tumbler and faked handkerchief, **you will need** a plastic beaker and five small silk handkerchiefs – two red, two yellow, and one green.

Use reef knots to join a red, yellow and green handkerchief **(1).** Then, starting at the red end, fold and roll them into a thin green bundle **(2).** It looks like just one handkerchief. Lay it on the table next to the unprepared red and yellow ones.

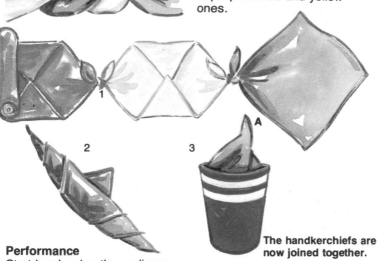

The handkerchiefs are now joined together.

Performance

Start by showing the audience that the beaker is empty. Then push the green bundle of handkerchiefs inside it, leaving corner **A** sticking out **(3).**

Pick up the extra red and yellow handkerchiefs and push them into the tumbler. Then make it vanish, using the faked handkerchief.

Pick up the breaker, grasp corner **A** and pull out sharply. The red and yellow handkerchiefs are now joined to the green!

47

The Magic Picture Frame

Materials
You will need two sheets of thick cardboard, four strips of balsa wood, a photo or picture, and an envelope large enough to hold the finished frame.

Preparation
Make a frame by sticking the balsa strips onto the large piece of card. Then paste the picture into the frame.

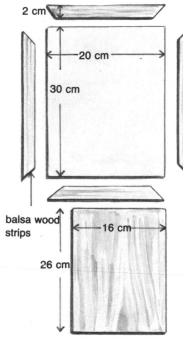

Cover the other piece of card with wood-grain wallpaper. It will form a flap fitting neatly into the frame to hide the picture.

Performance
Show the frame with the flap in place. Then after showing that the envelope is quite empty, place the frame inside.

Later, when you remove it, leave the flap in the envelope so that the picture is revealed.

Magic Painting

Tell the audience that you are going to turn a black and white picture into a colour one with the help of some special magic powder.

You will need a coloured picture to put into the frame and a black and white outline of the same picture which you paste onto the secret flap.

Do the trick described on the previous page. Sprinkle salt over the envelope, but call it 'ooffle dust' and say that it is extracted from all the colours of the rainbow.

Instant Photography

Draw a lens on the envelope and tell your audience that it is a new kind of camera and that the picture frame is the film. (Cover the secret flap with plain white paper.)

Put the 'film' into the camera and pretend to take a picture of one of your friends. Then open the envelope, leave the blank behind and bring out a really funny-looking portrait!

The Spooky Message

Force a card (see page 17), then ask your pet ghost to write the name of the chosen card in the magic picture frame.

Of course it is already there, hidden by the blank flap, but only you know that.

Make the writing look as spooky as possible.

Magic of the mind

Mind-reading or 'telepathy' tricks are always popular with an audience. You can introduce these tricks into any type of act to make people believe that you have special powers.

X-Ray Eyes

Preparation

Cut up about 30 pieces of thin card 9cm by 6cm, and draw a different design on each one.

Choose five of the cards and carefully memorize their order. Then hide them face down in the top of your **Enchanted Card Box,** instead of the secret flap.

When you close the drawer of the Enchanted Card Box, the cards you have memorized will fall down on top of the others.

Performance

Spread out the rest of the cards on your table. Then ask a friend to mix them up and place them face down in the box. Ask him to hand you the box, then close the drawer.

Pretend to think very hard, then slowly describe the design that is on the top card. Take it out and show everyone what amazing X-ray eyes you have!

You can repeat this with the other four cards – but it is best to name only two more in case someone challenges you to name one after you have finished.

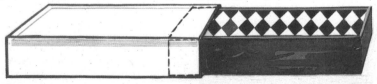

Zoo Prediction

Write a message – *'I predict that you will choose the elephant'* – seal it in an envelope, and ask someone to hold it.

Then hand out some pieces of card with the names of wild animals written on them, so that everyone can see they are all different. Collect them in a bag and shake it to mix them up.

Ask the person holding the envelope to choose a card and then open his envelope. He will be amazed to find that your prediction is correct!

How to do it
The secret is to use your Magic Changing Bag with one compartment already containing cards all saying 'Elephant'.

Place the other cards in the second compartment and change compartments when you ask a friend to choose a card.

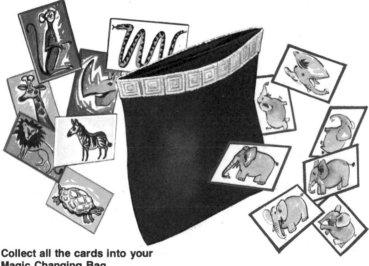

Collect all the cards into your Magic Changing Bag.

The Chosen Word

Hand a pocket dictionary to someone in the audience and ask another person to choose any page number. Announce that you are going to leave the room while they look up that page and write down the first word on it.

When you come back, pretend to think very hard, then slowly reveal the word, letter by letter.

How to do it
The crafty secret is to have a second dictionary in your pocket in which you look up the chosen page number!

A Production Box

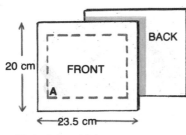

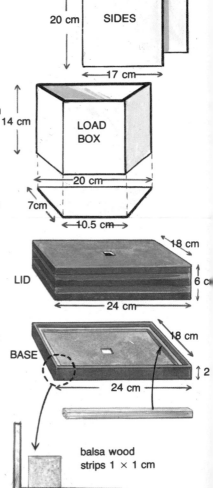

Materials: thick cardboard, sticky tape and four 1cm by 1cm balsa wood strips.

Front, back and side panels
Cut to the sizes shown.

Load box
Join all the edges with tape then glue along the dotted line **(A)** to the back of the front panel.

The lid
Cut a 2cm square hole in the centre.

The base
Should look like an upside-down lid. Glue the balsa strips inside it about 3mm from the edges to make a slot into which the panels fit. Cut a 2cm square hole in the centre.

Decorate the box with coloured paper.

Preparation
Assemble the production box then fill the load box.

Sprinkle some confetti into the box and put on the lid to keep everything secure.

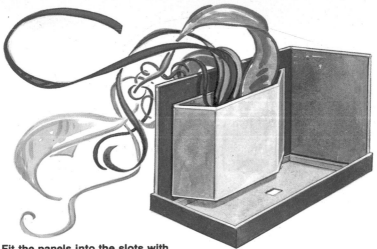

Fit the panels into the slots with the load box facing inwards.

Performance
Hold the box in your left hand, using the finger-hole to help balance it. Tell the audience that you are going to take the box apart to show that it is empty.
1. Take off the lid and place it upside down on the table.
2. Lift up the front panel with your right hand, put it behind the back panel, lift both together and lay them on the lid.

The load box will fit inside the lid, out of sight.
3. Remove the side panels and place them on top.
4. Spin the base on your finger and tip out the confetti.

Reassemble the box in reverse order – always keeping the load box facing away from the audience. Then spin the box, remove the lid and bring out all your hidden surprises!

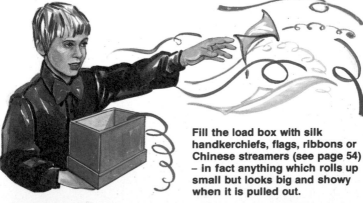

Fill the load box with silk handkerchiefs, flags, ribbons or Chinese streamers (see page 54) – in fact anything which rolls up small but looks big and showy when it is pulled out.

53

Chinese streamers

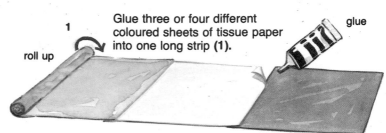

Glue three or four different coloured sheets of tissue paper into one long strip (1).

roll up

glue

Roll up the strip tightly, then cut small sections from it, about 2cm wide (2). Fasten the ends of five of these rolls under a

strip of cardboard, 2cm by 8cm (3), and pile the rolls together at one end (4). Stick on an extra band of tissue to stop them unrolling too soon.

2 cm

When you pull the streamers out of the production box, just break the extra band with your thumb and throw them towards the audience. Make sure you hold on tightly to the cardboard strip.

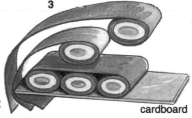

cardboard

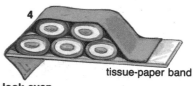

tissue-paper band

The streamers will look even better if you sprinkle confetti over the tissue paper before you roll it up.

A programme for a stage show

The stage show is the most difficult act of all. Think hard about your programme and practise it thoroughly beforehand. The routine below has lots of variety and takes about ten minutes to perform.

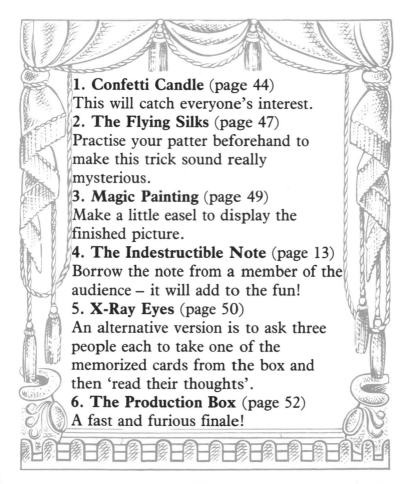

1. Confetti Candle (page 44)
This will catch everyone's interest.
2. The Flying Silks (page 47)
Practise your patter beforehand to make this trick sound really mysterious.
3. Magic Painting (page 49)
Make a little easel to display the finished picture.
4. The Indestructible Note (page 13)
Borrow the note from a member of the audience – it will add to the fun!
5. X-Ray Eyes (page 50)
An alternative version is to ask three people each to take one of the memorized cards from the box and then 'read their thoughts'.
6. The Production Box (page 52)
A fast and furious finale!

Arranging the stage

It is a good idea to use two tables so that you can work between them. Always keep your props in the same place, so that you can pick them up almost without looking. If your tables look too cluttered, you can keep small apparatus in the production box until you need it.

The **Confetti Candle** and ready-made paper cone. Don't forget the matches.

Silks for the **Flying Silks** trick, with corners held in place by the **Production Box**.

Wastepaper basket for disposing of your props as you finish with them.

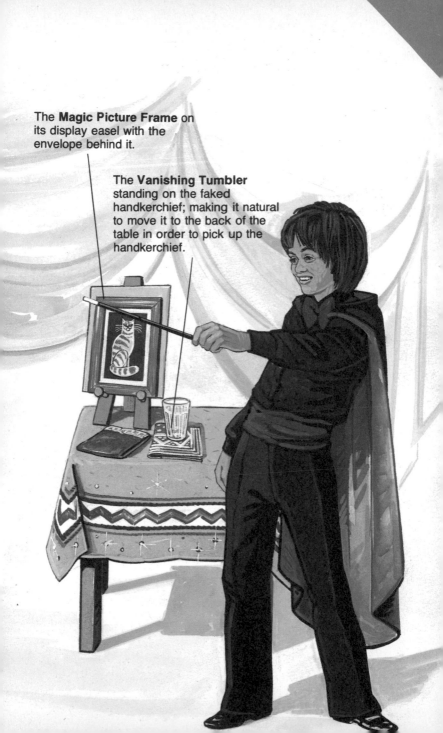

The **Magic Picture Frame** on its display easel with the envelope behind it.

The **Vanishing Tumbler** standing on the faked handkerchief; making it natural to move it to the back of the table in order to pick up the handkerchief.

Reference section

The golden rules of magic

A final word of advice as you start to become part of the wonderful world of magic: the only way to make progress is to keep on trying to improve. Practising and planning are both equally important.

Always be on the look-out for ways to make your tricks easier to perform and therefore more effective.

Read as much as you can, and try to watch as much magic as possible. You can always learn from other magicians – even from their mistakes!

Try to be original in the magic you choose to do, but remember that the best tricks are sometimes the oldest ones – provided that they are presented with style and personality.

Join a magic club or society (see page 59). You will find that other magicians are always ready to swop ideas and tricks.

In fact there are so many people interested in the art of magic that you are sure to find a welcome wherever you go.

1. Always practise well and prepare carefully before showing any trick in public.

2. Never tell anyone the secrets of your magic. Once they know how it's done, people will very quickly lose interest.

3. Never repeat a trick in front of the same audience, unless repetition is part of the trick. A second showing always lacks surprise, and just gives everyone another chance to find out the secret.

4. Don't go on too long, or try to show off by doing all the tricks you know. It's far better to do a few tricks really well, and leave your audience wanting more.

5. If something goes wrong, don't give up or be too apologetic. Laugh it off, and get on with the next trick as quickly as possible.

6. Always remember that magic is **FUN**. Show that you enjoy it and your audience will too.

Clubs and societies

Most large towns have a magic club, where magicians meet regularly, show each other their latest tricks, listen to lectures by famous magicians, and organize shows for the public.

Many of them have a junior section where some tuition is given.

A few of the larger societies are listed below:

The British Magical Society
Its headquarters and library are at the:
Birmingham and Midland Institute
9 Margaret Street
Birmingham B43 6EX.
For details write to:
Barry Gordon
Secretary
125 Whitecrest
Grear Barr
Birmingham B43 6EX.

The Magic Circle
84 Chenies Mews
London WC1
The Magic Circle has about 1,400 members and runs many functions throughout the year, including the Magic Circle Show just after Christmas at a London theatre.

Every second year it organizes the Young Magician of the Year Contest, open to magicians aged between 14 and 18.

It also has a clubroom, theatre, museum and library and meets every Monday.
For details write to:
John Salisse
Secretary
12 Hampstead Way
London NW11.

International Brotherhood of Magicians
This is a world-wide society based in Kenton, Ohio, USA., with about 10,000 members.

The British Ring organizes a convention, a picnic and a dinner every year, and publishes a monthly magazine *The Budget*.
For details write to:
W. G. Stickland
Secretary
The Wand
Ferndown, Dorset.

The Order of the Magi
Its headquarters are:
The Wesley Methodist Church
Royce Road
Hulme, Manchester 15.
For details write to:
Eric Wheeler
Hon. Secretary
2 Cedar Grove
Prestwich
Manchester.

Magic facts

The earliest record of a magician is in the Westcar Papyrus at the State Museum in East Berlin.

It describes a royal command performance before King Cheops, builder of the Great Pyramid, by a magician called Dedi, almost 5,000 years ago.

One of the earliest books about magic is *The Discoverie of Witchcraft* by Reginald Scot, published in 1584. Some of the tricks described in it are still performed today.

People from all walks of life have an interest in magic as a hobby.

The list of famous magicians includes: Orson Welles, Cary Grant, David Hemmings, Bill Bixby, Muhammad Ali, Evelyn Laye, J. B. Priestley, John Schlesinger, Prince Rainier of Monaco, Lord Louis Mountbatten, and HRH. Prince Charles.

The word magic comes from an Old Persian word *Magus;* meaning a member of the priestly caste among the Medes and Persians.

Probably the oldest trick in the world is the **Cups and Balls**. One ancient Roman word for magician was *Acetabularius*, meaning 'he who deals with vinegar cups'.

Magic suppliers

Many department stores and toy shops stock magic sets and individual tricks. But usually the range offered is limited. A good selection is to be found at:

Hamleys Magic Department
200 Regent Street
London W1.

For the widest range of magic apparatus however, you will have to go to a specialist shop or company.

If you cannot visit them they will be happy to send you a catalogue, so that you can choose what you want to order.

L. Davenport and Co.
51 Great Russell Street
London WC1.

International Magic Studio
89 Clerkenwell Road
London EC1.

Hughes House of Magic
The Grange, Willow Park
King's Lynn
Norfolk PE30 1EJ.

Supreme Magic Co. Ltd.
64 High Street
Bideford, Devon.

Magic Books by Post
29 Hill Avenue
Bedminster
Bristol BS3 4SN.

Booklist

If you have enjoyed this book, you will probably want to find out more about the different branches of magic.

Look for the books listed below in your local bookshop or library.

The Big Book of Magic by Patrick Page (Sphere Books)

The Royal Road to Card Magic by Jean Hugard and Fred Braue (Faber and Faber)

Magic and Showmanship by Henning Nelms (Dover)

The Complete Magician by Marvin Kaye (Macmillan)

Magic of the Masters by Jack Delvin (Hamlyn)

Magic for Beginners by Harry Baron (Kaye and Ward)

101 Magic Tricks by Guy Frederick (Piccolo)

The Beaver Book of Magic by Gyles Brandreth (Beaver Books)

Teach Yourself Magic by Robert Harbin (Hodder and Stoughton)

Close-up Magic by Harry Baron (Sphere Books)

Puffin Book of Magic by Norman Hunter (Penguin Books)

The Trade of the Tricks by John Wade (Elm Tree Books)

Magazines

Magazines are a useful guide to what is going on in the world of magic. Write to the addresses below for more information.

Abracadabra (weekly)
Goodliffe the Magician
Arden Forest Estate
Alcester
Warwickshire.

Magigram (monthly)
Supreme Magic Co. Ltd
64 High Street
Bideford, Devon.

Magic Info (monthly)
International Magic Studio
89 Clerkenwell Road
London EC1.

Genii (monthly)
Box 36068
Los Angeles
California 90036, USA.

Glossary

Apparatus: equipment specially designed to achieve a magical effect.

Close-up Magic: tricks with small objects performed at close quarters.

Effect: a trick as it appears to the audience.

Fake (sometimes spelt 'feke'): a gimmick, or a simulation of a real object.

Forcing: making a spectator choose a particular card, colour, number etc., without him realizing that it is not a free choice.

Foulard: a large silk square or headscarf.

Gimmick: a gadget or secret device which enables a trick to be performed; usually not seen by the audience.

Illusion: what the audience appears to see. A stage trick done with people or large animals.

Legerdemain: another word for sleight-of-hand.

Levitation: making someone or something float in the air without visible means of support.

Load: a concealed supply of items that is later produced.

Manipulation: sleight-of-hand performed on a stage.

Micro-Magic: a continental term for Close-up magic.

Misdirection: the art of distracting the audience's attention away from a secret move or a piece of apparatus.

Patter: what the magician says to distract or entertain the audience.

Production: making things appear, usually from an apparently empty container.

Props (short for 'Properties'): any apparatus or object used by a magician

Routine: the order of events during a trick. Also the arrangement of tricks for a show.

Set-up: the way props are arranged for a trick.

Silk: a handkerchief or foulard made of fine silk.

Sleight: A secret move made with the hands.

Sleight-of-hand: magic done by manipulation using the hands only.

Index